EMBRACE
WHERE YOU ARE

ON THE WAY TO WHERE YOU ARE GOING

Satise Roddy

Praise for *Embrace Where You Are on the Way to Where You Are Going*:

After reading *Embrace Where You Are on the Way to Where You Are Going* by Satise Roddy, I am completely and totally inspired and encouraged. It was as though God was speaking directly to me through the words on the pages.

Satise's message of God's perfect timing for your life, His amazing power, His faithful answer to prayer, His call to preparation, His armor of protection from the enemy, and complete abandonment and trust in Him is incredibly uplifting and points everyone directly to Jesus, our Savior. Her approach is real, honest and shows a humbleness that can only survive because Jesus is living inside of her.

She used an analogy about birds, who trust God for everything according to scripture, which validated and confirmed what God is doing in my own life right now! I had to stop and praise Him as I was reading.

Thank you for this sovereign, timely and important book for everyone's life. We need to walk in confidence and assurance that God must direct our paths and live in our hearts. This book provides an opportunity to learn how to do that, directs us to scripture, and most importantly, encourages us to be Holy Spirit led as we walk through this journey called life.

Lisa Stewart

Wow! I just finished reading *Embrace Where You Are on the Way to Where You Are Going* and I am rejuvenated! Satise has a beautiful insight on how to stay in sync with Christ while we're waiting for God's timing. And she wrote with such ease and depth that whether you're a seasoned Christian or a babe in Christ, you will fully understand the principles and be edified. God definitely used her to remind me of the extraordinary tools He's given us for our journeys. I'm going to reread. Thank you Satise!

Jaimie Blake

I am compelled to share how blessed and encouraged I am to have read, *Embrace Where You Are on the Way to Where You*

Are Going - written by Pastor Satise Roddy. This Godly inspired book spoke directly to my heart. It is definitely life changing!

Pastor Satise Roddy's message on His timing for our lives brought hope, encouragement and inspiration to me. His will and perfect timing for my life is everything! It reaffirmed to me the importance of being equipped with God's Power, mindful of my position in Him, staying prayerful and God's faithfulness in answering prayers, seeking His wisdom, understanding the need and reason for preparation time, being suited up in the Armor of God, listening to the voice of God and putting my heartfelt trust in Him.

Thank you Pastor Satise for this God-inspired timely and profoundly epic book. This book reaffirms that we all have a God given destiny and that we have a choice in choosing the route that we take to get to our destination. The pathway to our given destiny is through an intimate relationship and our heartfelt trust in God, through Jesus. This book, through sound biblical scripture and principles teaches us how to embrace where we are as we walk through our journey.

After reading this book, I am inspired, encouraged and ready to walk in the authority that God has given me!

Beverly Hess

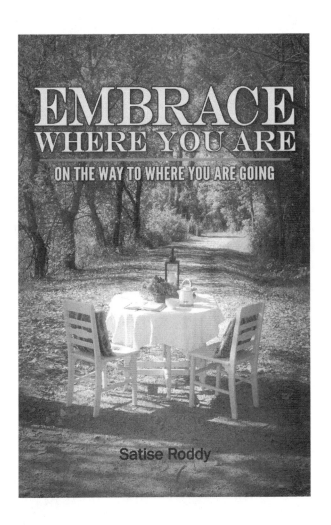

EMBRACE
WHERE YOU ARE
ON THE WAY TO WHERE YOU ARE GOING

Satise Roddy

Satise Roddy
MINISTRIES

<u>Embrace Where You Are</u>
On the Way to Where You Are Going

Published by Satise Roddy Ministries
Minneapolis, MN 55439 U.S.A.

Scripture taken from *The Holy Bible, New King James Version NKJV* and *The Holy Bible, New Living Translation Version NLT*

ISBN 978-0692627211
0692627219

www.satiseroddy.com

Cover Design: Sherry D. Photography
Minneapolis MN

Printed in the United States of America
First Edition 2016

1 2 3 4 5 6 7 8 9 10

CONTENTS

This book is dedicated:

To my Lord and Savior Jesus Christ, to whom I owe all that I am and could ever be. He is my Refuge and my Fortress, He is my Hope and without Him I can do nothing.

To my amazing husband Tim, whom I love with all my heart. Your unconditional love and support continues to bring me joy. Thanks Sweetie for being my mortal rock, and my biggest cheerleader. I am truly blessed to be your wife.

To my wonderful children, Perry and Rorye: I thank God for allowing me to be your mom. I smile when I think of you. I love you more than you could ever know.

To my siblings, Sharon and Delano: I love you both so much.

Acknowledgements

My deepest appreciation and love to my amazing husband, Tim whom I thank for his constant encouragement and support and without him this book would have been extremely difficult to write. Despite what he was doing at the time, he would stop to listen to my aha moments whenever I would get inspired. Thanks Sweetie, I love you more than more.

A huge shout out to my Aunt Marjorie who continues to inspire me with her love and words of encouragement. Thanks Auntie for cheering me on.

Lois, my cousin, you've believed in me from the beginning and always showed unconditional love for me. I love you to the moon and back.

My mom, Nell, I love and appreciate you.

My dear friends, mentors, and accountability Pastors Mauricio & Virginia Ruiz.

My God-Positioned Sisters (GPS), Anne, Germaine, Anita and Sheree, who have been with me when I have most needed you, and who continue to walk with me on this journey. No matter how far apart we are in distance, you will always remain in my heart. I love you all to life.

Much love and appreciation to Jaimie Blake. I'm blessed to have you as my sister in Christ, my friend. You inspire me.

My loyal sister/friend Bev. God knew!

Board Members of Satise Roddy Ministries, Tim Roddy, David & Beverly Hess

My Sister in Jesus and Tuesday morning Powerhouse Prayer Partner, Bianca Thomas. You are destined for greatness!

My Spiritual Daughters, you all know who you are.

DESTINED WOMEN'S Fellowship for your support.

And last, to all of you who continue to believe in what God is doing in and through me for His glory.

MY PRAYER

Father God I pray that as I complete this assignment, You will continue to give me godly wisdom, knowledge and understanding. I pray that my will is always aligned with what Your will is for me. May I walk in humility, boldness and love as You guide me. I pray that every person who reads this book will be inspired, encouraged and empowered to do what You have purposed them to do. May all know that You have a plan for their lives and with You all things are possible.

Heavenly Father may every word bring glory to You!

In Jesus' name.

FORWARD

Satise gave her manuscript to me to read. I was delighted. Delighted that she wrote the book and delighted that she would trust me to read it. I read it right away-- and then read it again. It is encouraging.

Through the years I have known her, she has always been an encouragement. She is real.

She is confident because of her relationship with Jesus.

She is an amazing example of God's handiwork.

I can't wait to pass it on to friends and acquaintances that may be helped by reading it and studying the scriptures cited.

Read her book, expecting to be confronted with truth… expecting to be encouraged… expecting to be empowered through her words and through scripture.

Trust in the Lord.

Don't allow distractions along your journey.

Stop.

Listen to the birds.

Prayerfully,

Karen Baden

ABOUT THE AUTHOR

Previously from the Los Angeles area, Satise now resides in Edina, MN with her amazing husband, Tim whom she loves with all her heart, and their two cherished Siberian cats. She is a mother to two grown sons, a Glamma, a sister, an ordained minister, a mentor, and a friend to many.

God lifted her out of the darkness. After struggling for years with depression and anorexia, God revealed Himself and delivered her. Through her struggle with identity, He showed her that her identity is in Him alone. Because of the grace of God, she is a cancer overcomer, and a walking example of His mighty healing power in all facets of life.

She knows firsthand of God's greatness, restoration and redemption. She has been crucified with Christ and Satise no longer lives, but Christ lives in her. The life she now lives in the body, she lives by faith in the Son of God, who loved her and gave himself for her (Galatians 2:20 NKJV).

In 2004, Satise answered the call of God on her life and has been ministering to the hearts of others ever since. She embraces her calling to minister to God's children in all areas of life. As a woman after God's own heart and with His strength she is able to encourage and motivate others – with a fun and energetic spirit. God has provided the platform for her to minister at churches, conferences, private groups, and public retreats. To God be the glory!

A magna cum laude undergraduate of University of Northwestern-St. Paul, MN where she earned her degree in Christian Ministries and a Certificate in Christian Counseling.

PROLOGUE

God gave me the desire to write a book some time ago. Recently, I decided to look through my journals and I realized the desire went back as far as 2004. Since that time, I can remember sitting down to write and I came up with nothing that was book worthy. The Scripture that was placed on my heart and I would hold on to was Habakkuk 2:2-3. I now see why these verses would burn so passionately in my heart from the time I can remember. God had given me the vision all those years ago, however it was for an appointed time. He has a way of giving us glimpses of things to come. But we must know that there are things we must learn in order to reach maturity to do what He is calling us to. Then the Lord answered me and said, "Write the vision and make it plain on tablets, that he may run who reads it, for the vision is yet for an appointed time; but at the end it will speak, and it will not lie. Though it tarries, wait for it; because it will surely come, it will not tarry (Habakkuk 2:2-3 NKJV). I believe the vision was for such a time as this. Now is the time.

As I sat down to write, I honestly had no idea what this book was going to be about, I had several ideas. Of course we know that our ways are not His ways, His ways are so much higher than ours.

My initial thought as to what I would write about was unclear. But somehow I knew that God would direct me. One thing I was clear about was that this book would not be my last. I was assured I would continue writing as I am led. This too was for an appointed time. There were many nights I would lay awake praying, asking God for His direction, after all, He is the One who put this on my heart. I knew that He would give me revelation; His timing is so perfect. Early one summer morning Anne, who is one of my best girlfriends, called me. Her words to me were, this is totally Holy Spirit led and she went on to say that God put me on her heart and she was to tell me that I needed to get started on my book. Wow, talk about confirmation. When we pray He answers! Anne told me she was going to drop a CD in the mail and that I needed to listen to it. A few days later I received the CD and as she encouraged, I listened to it over and over.

God revealed several things to me through this CD. As I listened intently, God ministered to me through this young lady. As she began to say things like; whatever you are passionate about, whatever excites you when you sit down with your friends, whatever it is that you would want to share with others is what you should write about. After hearing this, I thought for a moment and I began to discern the content of my book. It was then that I received the revelation. I am always super excited about telling others of the goodness of God, about inspiring, encouraging and empowering others to walk in the freedom that God has provided for each of us. That's my passion, that's my desire; that is what the content of my book would be about; simply to give them Jesus!

As you read, you will find that there is a great deal of Scripture inserted in the pages and this is done purposely because the Word of God is what brings meaning to my life; the Word of God is what excites me. I have to warn you though, I have been accused of using too much 'Christianese' (not sure that's a word). My response to that comment is always, "you should have heard me before I was transformed by the Word of God." Believe me Christianese is so much better.

Prayer: Father God, I pray that as your child reads this book they will not be conformed but transformed by the renewing of their minds and all will taste and see just how good You are in Jesus' name!

CHAPTER 1:

LIFE IS A JOURNEY

**"For I know the plans I have for you,"
says the LORD. "They are plans for good
and not for disaster, to give you a future
and a hope" (Jeremiah 29:11 NLT)**

A lot of prayer has gone into every page of
this book and every word has been
inspired by God. I pray that as you read
what God has downloaded in my heart

and Spirit to share with you, you feel a
fresh outpouring of His anointing. I pray
you feel His presence which will inspire,
encourage, and empower you to do and
be all He has called you to be. I pray that
you are transformed and no longer
conformed by the things that are not of
Him. He has plans for you, "plans for good
and not for disaster, to give you a future
and a hope" (Jeremiah 29:11 NLT). Our
hope is in Jesus and our future is eternal
life. Let's enjoy the journey... For the next
few chapters, I invite you to see yourself
the way God sees you. Your life will never
be the same. Now I encourage you to grab
a cup of tea or coffee, sit back, relax and
allow my God-inspired words to speak to
you in Jesus' name!

When I was younger, my friends and I
would always use the phrase, "life is a

trip". Actually I still hear this phrase being used today. Even though I would say it, I never really knew what it meant. I don't think I ever took the time to even care for what the actual meaning was or is. However as I mature in life, I believe it means that "Life is a journey"; at least that's what it means to me. So many ups and downs, mountains and valleys, twists and turns. We are all on a journey and we all have a destination; choose wisely the route you take. Your choice will determine your destiny. Your journey may not always be easy, but I can assure you that with Jesus, it will be easier. I've tried life with Jesus and I've tried life without Him. Believe me, it is so much better with Him. He will provide wisdom for us to walk through anything that tries to come against us. Because no matter what, we

have the victory in Jesus Christ. I've read
the end of the Book; Jesus wins! Put your
faith in Him, obey Him, reverence Him and
watch how He will move in your life and
your circumstances. Jesus is always there
to support, encourage and strengthen us
as we travel the road to our destiny. He is
the constant we can depend on and
always trust in. I do hope that as you
travel your own journey, you experience
an overabundance of joy. The kind of joy
that transcends anything you can think or
imagine.

Prayer: Father I pray your ministering
angels are encamped all around by sisters
and brothers that they may know that You
are with them as they travel the journey
to the destiny that You have for them.
May they know that they are not alone

and You are with them always, in Jesus'
name.

CHAPTER 2:

EQUIPPED WITH POWER

"For God has not given us a spirit of fear but of power, and of love and of a sound mind" (II Tim. 1:7 NKJV)

What I really love about this verse is that it never says we will not experience fear, only that God did not give us the spirit of fear. Once I grasped this truth I knew that if God did not give it to me, I didn't want it in my life. He has given us power, love and a sound mind. The word power describes delegated authority or influence. Therefore, authority and influence lives on the inside of each of us.

I am often told by many that they admire my confidence, my boldness, my courage and how real I am. These words literally make me smile because it gives me the opportunity to share Jesus. It gives me the opportunity to share hope. Who I am and what others see in me now is clearly because of His grace, His mercy and His love for me. My desire is that we would see things from God's perspective, recognizing His work in us. "I am what I am because of the grace of God" (I Corinthians 15:10 NKJV).

I walked around in the wilderness of depression for many years; not knowing or believing that I was loved. I know what it's like to feel hopeless, to feel beat down, to struggle with identity, to feel rejected and to want to give up. If you have felt any of these lies in any season in your life, then this book is for you. Wherever you may be on your faith journey, what I would like you to know is that you are loved and you are adored. God loves you so much that He gave His only Son so that you may have eternal life. His love is the Agape love. The unconditional, no strings attached love. No one, no matter how they try can love you like this. You are His masterpiece, His workmanship, created in Christ Jesus for good works. You are artfully created. You are destined for great things. "For we are His workmanship, created in Christ Jesus for good works, which God prepared

beforehand that we should walk in them"
(Ephesians 2:10 NKJV).

God has a plan for your life; He had a
specific purpose in mind when He created
you. In fact, He chose you before you
were formed in your mother's womb:

"Before I formed you in the womb I knew
you;

Before you were born I sanctified you;

I ordained you a prophet to the nations"
(Jeremiah 1:5 NKJV).

You must know that you were uniquely
created and there is not another person
on earth exactly like you. You are a big
deal and you have a special assignment to
accomplish. Get ready and do not give up
on what He has purposed you to do.

May I ask you, what is it that keeps you or has kept you bound? I encourage you to give it to Him. Really, He can handle whatever it may be. Go ahead, let go of all your worries and cares. Place them in the hands of our ever-loving Papa, for He cares for you. If you hold on to these things they have a way of robbing you of your joy and before long your circumstances began to take a toll on you. Believe me, I have been there and done that. Do not allow your circumstances to define you. We must not submit to our circumstances, but to the Lord who controls them. Let go and let God! Selah

Prayer: In the name of Jesus I bind any and everything that tries to keep you bound. You are free and who the Son sets free is free indeed. Walk in the power and freedom that has already been provided.

CHAPTER 3:

DON'T LET THE ENEMY ROB YOU OF YOUR POSITION

"The thief does not come except to steal, and to kill, and to destroy. I have come that they may have life and that they may have it more abundantly" (John 10:10 NKJV)

The enemy knows how much God loves you and his main purpose is to put conditions on you. His job is to distract

you from fulfilling your God-given
purpose. He knows that if he can distract
you long enough, the better his chances
are to get you to be on his team. But I am
binding the enemy in Jesus' name. God
has already placed you in a position of
power and the enemy knows that. Don't
allow mere distractions. You have been
equipped to walk in your power. You have
power, influence and authority - walk in it.
Don't let the enemy rob you of your
position by putting his conditions on you;
recognize his tactics. Stand up and take
your rightful position. Don't allow
anything that is not of God operate in
your life. "Look, I have given you authority
over all the power of the enemy, and you
can walk among snakes and scorpions and
crush them. Nothing will injure you" (Luke

10:19 NLT). Now that's some kind of power.

Prayer: Heavenly Father, help us to realize the enemy has no power nor authority in our lives. Because of the blood of Jesus we can cast Satan out, he is a liar from the pit of hell; we place him under our feet and he has been defeated in the name of Jesus.

CHAPTER 4:

STAY PRAYERFUL ALWAYS!

Never stop praying
(I Thessalonians 5:17 NLT)

Even though God has given you a vision, it's important to stay prayerful. Staying in communication with Him reassures you of His presence. There may be things that are happening around you that may not line up with what He has spoken to you. Be assured that the happenings around you are not as important as the things

happening in you. Don't listen to all the
chaos and noise, because God has said
that His Word will not return void. It will
accomplish the things He meant for it to
accomplish. We must continue to believe
by faith that if He has said it, He will bring
it to pass: "...Indeed I have spoken it; I will
also bring it to pass. I have purposed it; I
will also do it" (Isaiah 46:11 NKJV).

Then Elijah said to Ahab, "Go get
something to eat and drink, for I hear a
mighty rainstorm coming!" So Ahab went
to eat and drink. But Elijah climbed to the
top of Mount Carmel and bowed low to
the ground and prayed with his face
between his knees. Then he said to his
servant, "Go and look out toward the
sea." The servant went and looked, then
returned to Elijah and said, "I didn't see

anything." Seven times Elijah told him to go and look. Finally the seventh time, his servant told him, "I saw a little cloud about the size of a man's hand rising from the sea." Then Elijah shouted, "Hurry to Ahab and tell him, 'Climb into your chariot and go back home. If you don't hurry, the rain will stop you!'" And soon the sky was black with clouds. A heavy wind brought a terrific rainstorm, and Ahab left quickly for Jezreel. Then the LORD gave special strength to Elijah. He tucked his cloak into his belt and ran ahead of Ahab's chariot all the way to the entrance of Jezreel (I Kings 18:41-46 NLT).

I often wonder how Elijah felt when God told him there would be rain after the drought; Elijah trusted God and he began to pray for rain. Although, the rain did not come right away, he trusted, he believed and he did not give up. He knew that when God spoke it, it was not a matter of if the rain would come, but when. As Elijah prayed and waited, he was not without challenges; he faced many. If you are not familiar with this passage of Scripture, I would encourage you to read I Kings 17-18. You will be blessed. Just like Elijah, there will be challenges and obstacles that will present themselves to you, but not to worry;

'For I, the LORD your God, will hold your right hand,
Saying to you, 'Fear not, I will help you' (Isaiah 41:13 NKJV).

Pray for Others...

"Don't be selfish; don't try to impress others. Be humble, thinking of others as better than yourselves. Don't look out only for your own interests, but take an interest in others, too. You must have the same attitude that Christ Jesus had" (Philippians 2:3-5 NLT).

One of my favorite things to do is to pray for others. Even when they are unaware, even when I don't know the person personally. It doesn't matter because we all need prayer. I routinely go for a run four to five times per week. I pray over everyone whose path I cross. I pray over the people in their cars. I specifically stop on the overpass of the freeway where I run asking God to give each and every person peace. Whatever they may be going through, I ask for God's will in their lives. I pray for people and their homes, restoration in their families, their health, finances, and most of all I pray that all will come to know Jesus. Whatever God puts on my heart to pray, I pray. There are days when I may not feel up to running, but when I think of the commitment I have made to pray for others, I get inspired.

Pray According to His Will...

"And we are confident that He hears us whenever we ask for anything that pleases Him. And since we know He hears us when we make our requests, we also know that He will give us what we ask for" (I John 5:14-15 NLT).

We must pray according to His will and not our own. We are never to demand what we want or even expect God to conform to our wants; rather to align our prayers with the Word of God and what it is He wants for us. He listens to us as we pray with confidence according to His will. God knows what's best for us. As I pray, I ask God to prepare my heart to receive what it is He has for me. I only want His Best for my life and the lives of others.

Prayer: Heavenly Father, I am grateful that you have given me a heart for prayer. May the Holy Spirit continue to help me articulate as I intercede on behalf of others. I desire to pray Your word without ceasing for my life and the life of others in Jesus' name!

CHAPTER 5:

LISTEN TO THE BIRDS SING

**Give your burdens to the Lord,
and he will take care of you.
He will not permit the godly to slip and
fall (Psalm 55:22 NLT)**

I never realized how beautiful it is to listen to the sound of God's precious creatures. We can learn a lot from just listening to the birds singing and chirping. Music to my ears, an amazing melody. They fly around so carefree as if they don't have a worry in the world. "Look at the birds. They don't plant or harvest or store food in barns, for your heavenly Father feeds them. And aren't you far more valuable to Him than they are?" (Matthew 6:26 NLT). I want to challenge you the next time you're out and about, try listening to the sounds the birds make and when you do, I don't believe you will look at them the same. Just as I have, you will begin to develop a new appreciation for these precious creatures.

God cares about us so much that He gave us birds to listen to. The chirping and the singing, music to our ears if only we would allow ourselves the time to listen, to hear what they are saying; they tell us a lot.

You matter to God, He cares about every detail of your life. Nothing that you can possibly be experiencing can be too little or too big for Him. In fact, He cares so much that even the hairs on your head are numbered.

One summer day as I was on my daily run around the lake, I routinely stopped and sat on the dock to pray. This particular time as I prayed the very loud sound of birds singing made me take notice. I believe God used the birds to minister to me this day. It was like angels singing and God was revealing things to me. I thought about all the challenges I had been facing at that time in my life, all the stress that I had been under. Immediately, God revealed in a still small voice, "Satise, when did you stop hearing the birds sing?" There are times when we allow the world and all our circumstances to take over and we forget that we have a God who is so much bigger than all of the challenges we face. What might you be going through in this season of your life?

Think about the times when you were at your lowest, or what you thought to be your lowest. Did God fail to show up and provide what you needed at that time? Did He ever leave or forsake you? His Word says, He will supply all your needs according to His riches in glory in Christ Jesus! God is not a man that He should lie. If His word says it, He will do it. All His promises are Yes and Amen! No matter what challenge or circumstance you face, keep your focus on the Source, Jesus. Circumstances come and go but God remains the same. He is the same yesterday, today and always. I write this with much conviction. It is my years of walking with Jesus that this became my reality.

Peace, Calm and Joy, My Happy Place

I'm sure you know by now just how much I love running. My sister literally teased me by calling me Forest Gump. I love the sport so much and there was a time I ran so much that it became unhealthy, it literally posed a threat to me. You see at the time I was battling anorexia, so I was running like crazy and my food intake was not conducive to the amount of exercise I was doing. The doctors actually told me to stop running. ☺ Imagine being told to stop exercising.

You can say I was running on empty. What I know is that when I'm running on empty I'm not Trusting God. Awhile back I was experiencing some challenges with my health. I was going back and forth to the doctors, undergoing tests and they couldn't diagnose me. After a couple of weeks of this, as I sat in my screen room having God time I received a revelation and it was then that I realized what my diagnosis was; two words: over activity.

A lot of times we get so busy with things and they may be good things: ministry, helping others, or just doing. We forget to refuel and how many of you know that when you get so overwhelmed with things, you're actually running on auto-pilot. Not a good place to be. Running this way can cause us to trust in our natural self instead of putting the trust in God. This is neither honoring nor glorifying our Father.

I was being convicted of being on the go and being extremely exhausted. What was put on my heart was the Scripture: Be Still and Know that I am God. I had been meditating on this verse for a few days. It began to take on new meaning for me.

"Be still and know that I am God; I will be exalted among the nations, I will be exalted in the earth" (Psalm 46:10 NKJV). Being still, means to cease and desist. I equate being still to God being exalted, God being magnified, God being glorified. We have to take that time to be still, it's healthy both in the spiritual and the natural.

If you're wired the way I am, being still involves work. It's not always easy; we have to be intentional. In my life it requires giving up whatever endangers my relationship with God. Besides, in order to live effectively we must keep our eyes on Jesus. We stumble when we look away from Him to stare at ourselves or at the circumstances surrounding us. We have to remember we are running for Christ, not ourselves, and we must keep Him in sight always! If you have difficulty being still, pray and ask God to help you.

Spending time with God gives us new revelation. Being alone with Him is when He birthed the ministry He has called me to. When the Holy Spirit nudges me to slow down, I ask myself: What might God be trying to tell me? I had no idea God would use the very struggles I endured to speak to the hearts of others. When we are still it blesses us, it blesses those around us and it gives God the glory.

Prayer: Father God, I pray that we have the wisdom to know when it's time to be still to recharge, refresh and refuel. May we never put more importance on doing things for you that we forget to spend time with you. Give us discernment to know when things are good and when things are God. Help us to not miss out on the beauty of your creation. Help us to hear the birds sing and to listen when you may be trying to get our attention in speaking to us. This I pray in Jesus' name.

CHAPTER 6:

GOT WISDOM?

"Walk with the wise and become wise; associate with fools and get in trouble" (Proverbs 13:20 NLT)

Someone once told me that "association brings assimilation". As I matured I began to realize just how true this statement is. I can hear my mom telling me as a child, everyone is not your friend. I used to get so mad at her when she'd say that. As I look back I now know that was wisdom speaking. We should associate with those who are like-minded; those who are going places and wanting to become more like Jesus. "Don't team up with those who are unbelievers. How can righteousness be a partner with wickedness? How can light live with darkness?" (II Corinthians 6:14 NLT). I once heard a quote by Steve Maraboli:

"If you hang out with chickens, you're going to cluck. And if you hang out with eagles, you're going to fly."

Do you know that the fruit will tell you a lot about a person? It is wise to spend time with those who will pray for you, speak God's Word over you, edify you, and who will stand in agreement with who God says you are. These individuals should help propel you into the destiny that God has for you. Be very careful whom you choose to let in your close circle of friends. It's best to spend time with people you want to be like - friends tend to grow to resemble each other. I saw this quote on Facebook a while back and I just had to use it:

"Surround yourself with the dreamers and the doers, the believers and the thinkers. But most of all surround yourself with those who see the greatness within you, even when you don't see it yourself" (Edmunds Lee).

To that end, my advice to you is to use wisdom and discernment in determining who it is you should share your hopes and dreams with. Not everyone will understand your path and its okay because it not meant for everyone to understand. Not everyone understood the path of Jesus. He told His disciples He needed to go to Jerusalem to suffer and even though He explained this to them, Peter, who was having an emotional moment was not happy about this path. He truly loved Jesus and did not want this to happen to Him.

However, Jesus knew His purpose and did not allow any distractions, not even from His friends. In other words He was not moved by emotions but by what He was called to do. "Then Peter took Him aside and began to rebuke Him, saying, "Far be it from You, Lord; this shall not happen to You!" But He turned and said to Peter, "Get behind Me, Satan! You are an offense to Me, for you are not mindful of the things of God, but the things of men" (Matthew 16:22-23 NKJV).

Same with us, we have been given a purpose and we are not to get distracted but to fulfill our purpose. We are to stay focused; as we do this, we are blessed, others are blessed and God is glorified.

Prayer: Heavenly Father, I bind any and all distractions that try to come against our relationship with you. Anything that is not of you shall be eliminated out of our lives. Help us to keep our focus on You and on You only in Jesus' name!

CHAPTER 7:

PREPARATION TIME

"But those who wait on the LORD
Shall renew *their* strength;
They shall mount up with wings like
eagles,
They shall run and not be weary,
They shall walk and not faint" (Isaiah
40:31 NKJV)

I knew early on that I was called to the
fivefold ministry. Over 10 years ago my

pastor sat me down and asked me where I felt called in the ministry. I quickly said I felt called to be a pastor. It was from that time on this desire grew stronger and stronger. I was so excited about this revelation I had received from God. I was ready to preach or so I thought. As I look back on all those years ago, there is no way I would have been ready to preach to anyone. My pastors/mentors knew this. They took me under their wing, prayed for me, nurtured me, taught me and believed in what God was doing in and through me. Although God had given me this desire, there would be years of preparation. He knows when you are ready, His timing is perfect. Believe me you never want to step out prematurely. I always say that if it is not His timing, I am not stepping out. I am staying put until He has spoken. "The vision is for an appointed time" (Habakkuk 2:3 NKJV). You are anointed and appointed to do what He has called you to do. In His timing!

Dear friend, if God has given you a vision, it does not happen overnight; you must go through a process of waiting. Don't ever try to step out before it is time. When God plants the seed, allow it to grow within you. I encourage you to let it come to full term. Let's not birth it prematurely. While you're waiting for the vision to birth, take this time to establish a closer relationship with Him. Spend time in His Word, be transformed by renewing your mind. "And do not be conformed to this world, but be transformed by the renewing of your mind, that you may prove what is that good and acceptable and perfect will of God" (Romans 12:2 NKJV).

Really get to know our Heavenly Father.
Hear His voice; intimacy with Him is
priceless. Embrace where you are on the
way to where you're going and be
intentional about growing in the
knowledge of our Lord.

I know what it's like to have a desire to do
what God has called you to do and you
have to be in a season of waiting. Pray for
patience and peace as you wait. I worked
on a job/assignment for 3 ½ years that
was very challenging. I knew it was not a
good fit for me because I was not good at
it at all, but God sustained me. I also knew
that if God had me there, I had to
embrace it. It was a season of much
prayer and much believing and although
there were times of struggle, I never gave
up, I never stopped praying. After 3 ½
years my season there was over. Thank

You Jesus for giving me all I needed to complete the assignment with excellence. I prayed without ceasing. God gave me the grace to stay in the position but when that season came to an end, He lifted that grace and then gave me the grace to walk away. His ways are so much higher than our ways. If I had not listened to His voice, I would have walked away long before it was time and in doing so, the outcome would not have been the same. I left that assignment with peace and it was because I was obedient to stay there and trust Him even when I felt like giving up. Even when I felt I didn't have the strength to go on. I can relate to Paul when he expressed, "When I am weak, He is strong. His grace is sufficient for me" (II Corinthians 12:9 paraphrase). When nothing makes sense, and when circumstances seem more than you can handle, remember that God gives strength. We may be discouraged by events in life, but we must never give up hope in God's promises to us. Your turning point may be just ahead.

Embracing where you are is truly a humbling experience. As I write the words of this manuscript my faith is being stretched. Learning to rest in the waiting season with peace can only be done with God's peace, not the world's peace. Talk about tests, neither me nor my husband are employed at this time. This is a very challenging time for the both of us. But what we have decided to do is focus on our Source. His word says that "He will supply all our needs according to His riches in glory in Christ Jesus" (Philippians 4:19). We either believe it or we don't. We continue to embrace this season knowing that everything will turn around for the good for those of us who love Him and are called according to His purpose. We are reminded that circumstances are subject to change when God is involved. The joy of the Lord is our strength. Even in the storms or valleys of life, He is always there, He will never leave or forsake you. Grab hold of these truths as you learn to embrace where you are.

Do you remember when the Egyptians chased the Israelites to the Red Sea? There was no way for them to get around it, it appeared hopeless. Water was in front of them and Pharaoh and his army behind them. They were trapped; however, they did have options; to surrender, to fight, or to trust God. Of course we know that the best option would be to trust God and they did. God

made a way for them to cross. Hallelujah,
the victory was won!

And Moses said to the people, "Do not be
afraid. Stand still, and see the salvation of
the LORD, which He will accomplish for you
today. For the Egyptians whom you see
today, you shall see again no more
forever. [14] The LORD will fight for you, and
you shall hold your peace."

And the LORD said to Moses, "Why do you
cry to Me? Tell the children of Israel to go
forward. But lift up your rod, and stretch
out your hand over the sea and divide it.
And the children of Israel shall go on dry
ground through the midst of the sea. And I
indeed will harden the hearts of the
Egyptians, and they shall follow them. So I
will gain honor over Pharaoh and over all
his army, his chariots, and his horsemen.
Then the Egyptians shall know that I *am*

the LORD, when I have gained honor for Myself over Pharaoh, his chariots, and his horsemen." And the Angel of God, who went before the camp of Israel, moved and went behind them; and the pillar of cloud went from before them and stood behind them (Exodus 14:13-19 NKJV).

Do your part in fulfilling that vision and God will do His part. He has given you all you need to be successful. If you're not sure what to do. "Seek first the kingdom of God and His righteousness and all things will be added to you" (Matthew 6:33 NKJV). There are times when you may think God has anointed you to do something but you can't seem to get in a position to do it! Know that God is positioning you right now; He's preparing you for such a time as this. Don't give up, keep moving in Him. Rely on Him to open the doors He wants you to walk through. In His timing He will promote you to where He wants you to be. "Humble yourselves before the Lord, and he will lift you up in honor" (James 4:10 NLT).

I happened to be on Facebook one day and ran across something that I really liked:

>When the idea isn't right
>
>God says No
>
>When the time isn't right
>
>God says SLOW
>
>When you're not ready
>
>God says GROW
>
>When everything is right
>
>God says GO

"No eye has seen, no ear has heard,
and no mind has imagined
what God has prepared
for those who love him" (I Corinthians 2:9
NLT).

Someone once said to me that she
couldn't believe how long I had been
struggling to get my ministry going. She
mentioned how puzzled she was because
she knew that I was always so faithful and
diligent in praying and yet nothing
seemed to be happening. I thought about
what she had said for a few days and I
realized what I was going through was not
a struggle at all but a refining process, a
preparation season. I made a choice
during this time and that was to choose to
see things from God's perspective. He was
simply shaping me, molding me and

equipping me and preparing me for the things He had for me to do. My God was not going to send me out before it was time and definitely not without a hedge of protection all around me.

Weeks later, I invited my friend to join me for a cup of tea and I began to share this with her. Right then and right there I began to thank my Heavenly Father for keeping me from stepping out ahead of Him. If His anointing is not on it, I want no part of it. It's time when He says it's time. Hallelujah!!

Choose to see all the beautiful things that God is doing in your life while you're in this season; thank Him for this time in your life. Trust me, He knows what He is doing. Everything He is doing will be used for His glory. I once shared with a friend and dear sister in Christ about a time when God had me in a position of waiting. She used an analogy which I thought was awesome and very timely. So allow me to share it with you. My friend used the analogy of one being in the military and waiting for their marching orders from the general before going to battle. If you step out before receiving the orders you risk the chance of stepping out into enemy territory and getting blown up. The moral to this story is never step out before you receive your orders from God. He knows when it's safe for you to step out. Always remember that when you're in a waiting season; you're in training. God will make a way; His timing is perfect.

Don't let temporary setbacks keep you from stepping up. Obstacles can become stepping stones. You have been setup with everything you need to be successful in the things God has purposed you to do. God always leads us to triumph. Keep walking in your God given purpose. I don't know what stumbling blocks or what obstacles you may be facing at this very moment, but what I do know is that God is with you. He goes before you to make your path straight and He is your rear guard. Do not fear; He has your back. You are more than a conqueror in Christ Jesus! "Yet in all these things we are more than conquerors through Him who loved us." (Romans 8:37 NKJV). It is written.

Prayer: Heavenly Father, help us to learn to wait on your timing. My desire is to submit and obey you, to wait on Your timing and to never step out without hearing from You. I realize that You only want Your best for me and my desire is to never step out prematurely. This I pray in Jesus' name!

CHAPTER 8:

SUIT UP

"Therefore, put on every piece of God's armor so you will be able to resist the enemy in the time of evil. Then after the battle you will still be standing firm. Stand your ground, putting on the belt of truth and the body armor of God's righteousness. For shoes, put on the peace that comes from the Good News so that you will be fully prepared. In addition to all of these, hold up the shield of faith to stop the fiery arrows of

the devil. Put on salvation as your
helmet, and take the sword of the Spirit,
which is the word of God. Pray in the
Spirit at all times and on every occasion.
Stay alert and be persistent in your
prayers for all believers everywhere"
(Ephesians 6:13-18 NLT)

Have you ever gotten dressed to go out to
a special event without being fully
clothed? Just imagine being really decked
out but forgetting to bring your shoes if
it's cold, I mean cold as in a Minnesota
winter. Most of you cannot even imagine
how cold it gets in the midwest. Well let
me just say, you don't know cold until
you've lived through a winter in the Land
of 10,000 lakes. When I was in California I
loved getting all dressed up to go to an

event. Honestly if I forgot a jacket it really was no big deal. However being in Minnesota if you even thought to go outside without a jacket, you would never let it happen again. As I thought of leaving an item of clothing at home, I thought about the Armor of God. Friends the Armor is not a fashion statement and you never want to leave home without being fully clothed in its entirety. The Word says to put on the whole Armor. God provided this for us because He knew we would need it. This armor will guard us from the attacks of the enemy. I've learned that the bigger the assignment, the stronger the attacks. I'm keeping my armor on and even sleeping in my gear. The Word says to put on the whole armor of God; not part of it. We have the weapons we need to defeat Satan and anything else that tries to come against us. But in order to do this we have to be armed and ready at all times. Don't leave home without it.

Prayer: Father God, thank You for providing all that we need to come against spiritual warfare. We realize we do not wrestle against flesh and blood but against principalities and because You have provided the Whole Armor, we have the victory in Jesus' name!

CHAPTER 9:

THE VISION IS FOR YOU

**To everything there is a season,
A time for every purpose under heaven
(Ecclesiastes 3:1 NKJV)**

I must share with you a valuable lesson
God taught me. God gave me a vision and
I was so excited, I couldn't wait to share
this revelation with a friend of mine. I
invited her for tea to share this with her.
My passion was through the roof. I just

knew my friend was going to share in this excitement. As I began to share, the look I got was not at all what I expected. She looked at me as if I had said something horrible. I was crushed. Of course when I left her, I began to pray asking God did I hear Him wrong. But what God revealed to me was that the vision and desire that was put in my heart was for me. Others may not be able to see it because God did not give it to them. Maybe you have experienced this. You honestly cannot share everything with everyone. Pray, asking God who you should share with, if anyone. Not everyone will support you and how could they? God did not give them the vision, He gave it to you so I encourage you to surround yourself with those who will propel you into your destiny. Choose friends who are in agreement with who God says you are, who will support the vision He has given you: those who are for you and not against you; those who will encourage you and pray for you. When Jesus was being transfigured on the Mount; He only took Peter, James and John with Him. In other words the inner circle of those closest to Him. "Now after six days Jesus took Peter, James, and John his brother, led them up on a high mountain by themselves; and He was transfigured before them. His face shone like the sun, and His clothes became as white as the light" (Matthew 17:1-2 NKJV).

Not everyone is meant to go everywhere you go or be with you as God moves you from glory to glory.

I'm sure many of you have seen the Wizard of Oz. Dorothy was on a journey, she was determined to get to her destination. Remember how many people she encountered on her journey? Do you recall how many of those people reached the destination with her? People are put in your life sometime for a season and a reason, it doesn't necessarily mean they're supposed to stay the course.

To that end, my advice to you is to use wisdom and discernment in determining who you should share your hopes and dreams with. Not everyone understands your path.

It's Okay to Dream

What did you want to be when you grew up? Can you remember what you dreamed you'd be? We all have dreams and aspirations and there are times when we allow life's circumstances to cause our dreams to lay dormant inside of us. I vaguely remember my childhood dreams, I do remember that I had several and honestly when I grew up, I don't recall really having the desire to do any of those things. But as an adult, God placed a dream in my heart and when He places hopes and dreams within our heart, He wants to fulfill them for His purpose.

This is the time to let God's Word serve as inspiration. His Word is powerful, and is meant to lift us up in times like these. If you have a dream in your heart, I encourage you to pray about it asking for His guidance. You will know if this is something He has placed within you. And if so, He will grant you the desires of your heart and fulfill your purpose. It may seem impossible to man, but know that with God, all things are possible. So believe and

receive; when God gives you a dream He
can make it a reality.

REJECTION:

Don't fear rejection; it comes with the
territory. I'm sure you've heard the
phrase, "rejection is God's protection or
redirection." When I was young, early pre-
teens to be exact, I thought I wanted to
pursue a musical career. I had the gift, but
I lacked the passion it took to succeed. I
had a person in my life who would
manage my career; this person was also
someone that was close to me, someone I
love and trusted. I would go on several
auditions which to me was no fun at all. I
recall this one specific audition which
would be a very pivotal point in my life. I
sang my little heart out, I did my best but I
did not make the cut, I was not advanced
to the second round. My manager's words

to me rang over and over in my head as this person said to me, "I knew you would not make the cut because you are not star material." Ouch, that really hurt me. That would haunt me for years. I became afraid to perform in front of an audience for fear of rejection but even more if I were rejected what would my manager say or think of me?

REDIRECTION:

I met a lot of people when I was in the music industry - people who were not what they appeared to be. Because I was at such a vulnerable state, I could have gotten connected with people that were not the best for me... I believe even though God gifted me with vocal ability, the direction I was headed was clearly not His best for me. I lost interest in pursuing a career in music in the secular world.

Praise God my steps were and continue to be ordered of the Lord.

Prayer: Father God, I pray that my will is aligned with what Your will is for me. I pray that whatever I am believing for, if it is not of you, you will remove it from my life and prepare my heart to receive whatever it is You have for me, in Jesus' name!

CHAPTER 10:

LISTEN TO HIS VOICE AND OBEY HIS COMMAND

**Trust in the LORD with all your heart,
And lean not on your own understanding
(Proverbs 3:5 NKJV)**

Years ago God told me that I would have a women's ministry. I wasn't sure that this was something I'd want to do. I loved the speaking part of the ministry where I would go out minister to women at different retreats, conferences, etc. in an evangelistic role. Go out preach Jesus and move on. But clearly, this was not all He has for me. I would see His hand at work in my life as He continues preparing me to shepherd women. God prompted me to launch DESTINED WOMEN, a women's fellowship in 2013. This is a thriving ministry where I inspire, encourage and empower women to walk in the freedom God provided for them. Many women's lives are being changed because of my being obedient in what He purposed me to do.

I am originally from California but in 2005 I met and fell in love with my amazing husband, Tim and in 2007 I moved to Minnesota and we were married. Tim knew my passion and he is and always has been very supportive in what God is calling me to do. Being in a new state, it was difficult to gain credibility as a minister. People tend to stick with who they know. So my ministering invitations weren't exactly rushing in. My dear husband would tell me to stop waiting on others to invite me to minister. In fact he said I should start my own ministry. He would tell me this for years. Even though I knew my sweet husband was right, I had to wait for the appointed time. It wasn't until 2012, I was speaking with a good friend whom I mentioned earlier; this friend asked me when was the last time I ministered. I believe our conversation was in July. I went on to tell her that I hadn't ministered since March. She couldn't believe it. She said that when I was in California I was ministering all the time, she asked what happened. I shared with

her that no one was inviting me to speak.
And like a true girlfriend she asked,
"Satise when have you ever let someone
stop you from doing what God has called
you to do?" She said the Satise she knew
would never do such a thing. It was almost
as if something clicked inside me. It was at
that moment, I heard a still small voice say
to me: Now is the time. "The LORD is good
to those who depend on him, to those
who search for him" (Lamentations 3:25
NLT).

Wow, all those years when I didn't feel
ready was because it was not His timing,
but as soon as it was, He told me to go out
and possess the land. Women are hurting,
women need Jesus. I have prepared you
for such a time as this. When it is His
timing, it doesn't matter who's against
you. When others will not open a door, He

will open a door no man can shut. He will send the people who will support you, people you never knew existed. If God is for you, nothing can stand against you. "What shall we say about such wonderful things as these? If God is for us, who can ever be against us?" (Romans 8:31 NLT).

Just like He is preparing me for things to come, He is preparing you, my friend. He has work for you to do. Be diligent in finding out what it is and be obedient in what He is showing you and telling you to do. But also follow His lead!

Prayer: Heavenly Father, thank you for providing me with wisdom, knowledge and understanding to do Your will. Thank You for going before me to make my path straight and for being my rear guard in Your name, Amen.

CHAPTER 11:

WHOSE VOICE ARE YOU LISTENING TO?

**Your own ears will hear him.
Right behind you a voice will say,
"This is the way you should go,"
whether to the right or to the left (Isaiah
30:21 NLT)**

Who you allow to speak in your life can
make all the difference. Adam and Eve in
the Book of Genesis knew exactly what

God told them to do. But instead of trusting Him, they decided to listen to the voice of the serpent which caused the fall of man. You see, when God tells you to do something, do not allow someone or something to come along and redirect you. "...they follow Him because they know His voice. They won't follow a stranger; they will run from him because they don't know his voice" (John 10:5 NLT). It saddens me to see others miss out on what God has called them to do because they trust man instead of God. Scripture tells us that "it is better to trust in the Lord than to put confidence in man" (Psalm 118:8 NKJV).

There was once a woman (in leadership) who told me that the Holy Spirit revealed to her that I should become ministry partners with her. She said that I should

uproot the ministry God had called me to
and combine it with hers. I informed her
that I did not hear that from God, God had
not revealed that to me. Be careful, I don't
think God will reveal something about
your ministry to someone else without
revealing it to you or at least giving you
peace about it. Praise God, I heard His
voice and did not listen to the voice of
others and neither should you. He has an
amazing plan for your life and it is not just
for you but to bless others and to glorify
Him. Do not forfeit your God-given vision
by listening to what others think you
should be doing. I'm am not saying that
others are all the time deliberately trying
to sabotage you or your God-given
purpose because they may really feel that
they are speaking truth to you. What I am
saying is to make sure you are hearing
from God and that you are not missing out

on what He is saying to you. Be careful friends in not allowing the opinions of others to hold you back from your God-given purpose. Jesus knew what His purpose was and He was not going to allow anyone to interfere.

There will always be distractions that will try to hinder you from your purpose, sometimes in the form of those closest to you. But remember God is God; with Him all things are possible. He has equipped you with all you need to do and be who He has called you to be.

Stay in Your Lane

There are times when we are so attracted to what others are doing that it can cause us to miss the mark on what it is we're to be doing. Have you been there? I certainly have. When I was called to the ministry all

those years ago, there were several things
that I wanted to do, but by the grace of
God I soon realized that I would be setting
myself up for failure if I tried to do it all.
We are all blessed with gifts and talents
and it's imperative that we learn what our
gifts are. Years ago I was in a runner's club
and whenever we were instructed to run
around the track we all had our specific
lanes. At times one of us would get
distracted and cross over into someone
else's assigned lane. This would then
throw everything off, causing others to
lose focus on their original assignment.
The same analogy can be used in our life.
If we are not focused and intentional
about our own assignment, we can easily
cross over into someone else's, missing
what it is we're supposed to be doing. We
have been blessed with specific gifts so
that we may bring glory to God. If we are

not being true to who we've been called to be, we are not glorifying the One who created us.

Don't expect others to do what only God can do. Take the pressure off. God is your Source.

When I relocated to Minnesota, my desire was to get connected with others in ministry so that they would get to know my heart, my love for Jesus and my calling and the passion I had. It wasn't so easy. I have had many doors closed because I do not have a Master's Degree in Divinity (M.Div). It was difficult to gain credibility without that degree. One thing I know for sure that when God opens a door no one can close it. He will open the right door for you at the right time. Where He guides, He will provide. I'm not against formal education at all, in fact, if that is your desire and God opens the door for you "go for it". I was blessed to attend an amazing university to obtain a B.S. in Ministries and certificate in Christian Counseling. I am saying that it doesn't always matter how many degrees one has, nothing and no one can contend with the Master's Degree. I have such respect for those who have formal education. In fact, I would like to someday return to pursue my M.Div if it's God's will.

Prayer: Father, help me to keep my eyes on You as I run the race that is set before me and in doing so may You receive all the glory.   Amen.

CHAPTER 12:

I DON'T WANT TO GIVE MY TESTIMONY

And they overcame him by the blood of the Lamb and by the word of their testimony, and they did not love their lives to the death (Revelation 12:11 NKJV)

Many years ago, I was asked by my former pastor to share my testimony on the platform one Sunday. I literally told my pastor I would pray about it and let him know. Truth was, I was terrified. I flashed back to my days of performing and immediately I thought about how I'd feel if I were rejected, or what if no one listened or even cared about what I would have to say? I was afraid to stand in front of a crowd. After praying about it, God showed me that this was not a performance. He showed me that I am to minister to the heart of others. Once He revealed this to me, I had to share about the goodness of God. Think of all the lives that could be delivered and set free by seeing what God had done in my life. Besides, this was not about me, but to glorify God. I would share my testimony that Sunday long ago and many were delivered and not only were others set free, but I was set free. When God calls us to do something, we don't get to pick and choose but to be obedient with a grateful heart. Sharing what God has and is doing in your life provides hope for someone who may have or may be struggling. God is a God of hope and He is no respecter of persons. What He's done for you, He can and will do for others. Go tell somebody! When God has spoken, nothing can stop you!

"No weapon formed against you shall prosper,
and every tongue which rises against you in judgment you shall condemn.
This is the heritage of the servants of the LORD, and their righteousness is from Me," says the LORD (Isaiah 54:17 NKJV).

I'm not who I was!

A while back I had the opportunity to visit
a place that I had not been in almost
twenty years. I was last in this place at a
time in my life when I was at an all-time
low. As you read, you will realize that I
obviously wasn't walking with God at the
time. When I was there all those years
ago, I was in a state of major depression.
And being there made the depression
worse. Oh yes, I was reading my Bible but
not living it. When I returned not long ago,
I found that this place was the same, the
people were the same, and nothing much
had changed. But I had changed. God had
done a work in me and this time when I
was there, I returned with a new song in
my heart. I had the opportunity to be a
light, to reflect Jesus and to cast out that
spirit of depression. I was so blessed that I
got to reflect Jesus, I got to show that with
Him life can be transformed and our

minds can be renewed. I was able to show that I am not who I was!

I simply love the story of Esther (Esther chapters 3-8), a young Jewish girl who had been given a huge assignment. Because of where she came from; an adoptee and an orphan, she was the least likely to accomplish this assignment. But even so, she was crowned Queen of Persia. Haman second in command manipulated the king to sign a decree to execute all the Jews in the land. Clearly, the king was unaware that Esther, his queen, was a Jew. Esther would need to defend the Jews and go before the king to plead the case for her people. This was a very difficult task as in those days no one approached the king unless the king himself had summoned them; death was the penalty. Oh no, this did not stop her. Esther completed her assignment, she was used by God to save her people. So you see it didn't matter what her background was, it didn't matter where she had come from. Just as God set her up to do great things, He is doing the same for you. You are called for such a time as this. What is it that He is telling you to do? Think about it, pray about it and get moving.

Prayer: Heavenly Father, thank You for never leaving or forsaking me. May I continue to be transformed by renewing my mind with Your word. Continue to equip and prepare me to do what you have called me to do for your glory in Jesus' name.

CHAPTER 13:

TRUST(.), TRUST(?), TRUST(!)

**"Trust in the LORD with all your heart;
do not depend on your own
understanding.
Seek his will in all you do,
and he will show you which path to
take" (Proverbs 3:5-6 NLT)**

Can you think of a time when you were
facing a challenge that seemed impossible
to get through? You knew going in that

without a doubt you trusted God. As
things progressed, seemingly getting
worse instead of getting better, you began
to question whether or not you were
really trusting God at all. As you were
going through the storm (key words;
"going through") and made it to the other
side because God always brings us
through, you realized yes, you trust Him!
Do not focus on the circumstances but on
God who engineers your circumstances.

I am reminded of our friend Peter; as long
as he kept his eyes on Jesus, he trusted
that he could walk on water and he did
until he began to focus on the
circumstances surrounding him. He then
began to doubt, he became fearful and he
began to sink.

"Yes, come," Jesus said.

So Peter went over the side of the boat
and walked on the water toward Jesus.
But when he saw the strong wind and the
waves, he was terrified and began to sink.
"Save me, Lord!" he shouted.

Jesus immediately reached out and
grabbed him. "You have so little faith,"
Jesus said. "Why did you doubt me?"
(Matthew 14:29-31 NLT).

Let's choose to keep our eyes on Jesus
and not what seems to be causing a
distraction around us. If we continue to
keep our eyes on the Source, we will be
able to walk on water.

Prayer: Father I pray that as I grow in the
knowledge of knowing You, my faith is
strengthened and may come to be more

and more like you. I pray that I do not take my eyes off You, no matter what the circumstances and no matter what happens around me. You are my Source and I will keep my eyes on YOU, in Jesus' name!

CHAPTER 14:

SET-BACKS CAN BE SET-UPS FOR COMEBACKS

In his kindness God called you to share in his eternal glory by means of Christ Jesus. So after you have suffered a little while, he will restore, support, and strengthen you, and he will place you on a firm foundation (I Peter 5:10 NLT)

In 2005 I was diagnosed with a very aggressive form of breast cancer. The prognosis did not look good and the doctors didn't expect me to make it. I would immediately start some very aggressive treatment consisting of eight months of chemotherapy and two months of radiation. I was basically bed-ridden for the majority of 2006. Even though this was a very challenging time, I chose to hold on to the promises of God while staying faithful to His Word. I used this time to go deeper with Him, to get to know Him more intimately.

While I was going through treatment, I specifically remember one night lying in bed in a great deal of pain and unable to sleep. I had a vision as I was laying there; I was sitting in a church with my best friends whom I thought were sitting unusually close to me. But when I reached out to touch them, they seemed so far away. We were looking toward the front of the church and the more we watched, I would realize that we were at a memorial service. I looked on very intently to find that we were at my memorial service. It was at that moment I sat straight up in my bed. The Scripture that came to me in that moment was John 11:4, "This sickness is not unto death, but to glorify God so the Son of God may be glorified in it" (John 11:4 NKJV). I knew at that moment that I was going to be okay.

God showed me that my work here on earth is not done. That was almost 10 years ago and my desire is to bless others while glorifying Him in the process. It's not over until He says it's over.

A few years later, God revealed to me what that vision was about. That memorial service was in fact mine; it was when I truly died to myself and I began to let go and let God be in control of my life.

There are times when life throws you a curve-ball, things you don't expect, things you don't want; but we must never give up. Continue to trust and do all you can to fulfill your purpose no matter what gets in the way.

Prayer: Heavenly Father, I thank You for being our Healer. You said in Your Word that many are the afflictions of the righteous but you will deliver us out of them all. You said that we shall live and not die and declare the works of the Lord. You are Jehovah Rapha, Jehovah Jireh, Jehovah Shalom. You are the Alpha, The Omega, The Beginning and The End. You are the Author and the Finisher of our

Faith. You are our peace, our joy and we thank You in Jesus' name!

CHAPTER 15:

BE THANKFUL

Do not be anxious about anything, but in everything by prayer and supplication with thanksgiving let your requests be made known to God (Philippians 4:6 NKJV)

Ask God to give you the wisdom to know what to do and the courage/boldness to step out and follow through on what He has purposed you to do. It will take faith,

focus and follow through. Have the faith
to know that God will do what He said He
will do. This does not mean you sit around
and do nothing, waiting for Him to do it
all. We cannot expect God to do for us
what He wants to do through us.

Prayer: Father, we thank You for loving us
and calling us for such a time as this in
Jesus' name!

Remember if He has called you to it, He
will equip you with what you need to do
it.

FINAL NOTE

I pray this book has blessed you above
and beyond. I pray that you are now
inspired, and encouraged more than ever
to walk in the power, authority and
influence that God has provided for you.
You are absolutely amazing with an
amazing hope and future. I encourage you
to embrace where you are on the way to
where you're going.

INVITATION

I am not sure where you are in your
relationship with God. If you have not yet
accepted Him as your Lord and Savior and
you are ready to give your life to Him; I
invite you to reach out to Him right now.
He is waiting with open arms to embrace
you. I promise you that making this
decision will transform you and your life
will never be the same. In Jesus' name!

**If you openly declare that Jesus is Lord
and believe in your heart that God raised
him from the dead, you will be saved
(Romans 10:9 NLT).**

SCRIPTURE REFERENCES

Taken from the New King James and New
Living Translation Versions of the Bible

I have been crucified with Christ; it is no
longer I who live, but Christ lives in me;
and the life which I now live in the flesh I
live by faith in the Son of God, who loved
me and gave Himself for me **(Galatians
2:20 NKJV). About the Author, Page 20**

"Write the vision and make it plain on
tablets that he may run who reads it, for
the vision is yet for an appointed time; but
at the end it will speak, and it will not lie.
Though it tarries, wait for it; because it
will surely come, it will not tarry
**(Habakkuk 2:2-3 NKJV). Prologue, Page
24**

For I know the plans I have for you," says the LORD. "They are plans for good and not for disaster, to give you a future and a hope **(Jeremiah 29:11 NLT). Chapter 1, Page 29**

For God has not given us a spirit of fear but of power, and of love and of a sound mind **(II Tim. 1:7 NKJV). Chapter 2, Page 35**

But by the grace of God I am what I am, and His grace toward me was not in vain; but I labored more abundantly than they all, yet not I, but the grace of God *which was* with me **(I Corinthians 15:10 NKJV). Chapter 2, Page 36**

For we are His workmanship, created in Christ Jesus for good works, which God prepared beforehand that we should walk in them **(Ephesian 2:10 NKJV). Chapter 2, Page 38**

"Before I formed you in the womb I knew you;
Before you were born I sanctified you;
I ordained you a prophet to the nations"
(Jeremiah 1:5 NKJV). Chapter 2, Page 38

The thief does not come except to steal, and to kill, and to destroy. I have come that they may have life and that they may have it more abundantly **(John 10:10 NKJV). Chapter 3, Page 41**

Look, I have given you authority over all the power of the enemy, and you can walk among snakes and scorpions and crush them. Nothing will injure you **(Luke 10:19 NLT). Chapter 3, Page 42**

Never stop praying. **(I Thessalonians 5:17 NLT) Chapter 4, Page 45**

Calling a bird of prey from the east,
The man who executes My counsel, from
a far country.
Indeed I have spoken it;
I will also bring it to pass.
I have purposed it;
I will also do it **(Isaiah 46:11 NKJV).**
Chapter 4, Page 46

Then Elijah said to Ahab, "Go get
something to eat and drink, for I hear a
mighty rainstorm coming!"

So Ahab went to eat and drink. But Elijah
climbed to the top of Mount Carmel and
bowed low to the ground and prayed with
his face between his knees.

Then he said to his servant, "Go and look out toward the sea."

The servant went and looked, then returned to Elijah and said, "I didn't see anything."

Seven times Elijah told him to go and look. Finally the seventh time, his servant told him, "I saw a little cloud about the size of a man's hand rising from the sea."

Then Elijah shouted, "Hurry to Ahab and tell him, 'Climb into your chariot and go back home. If you don't hurry, the rain will stop you!'"

And soon the sky was black with clouds. A heavy wind brought a terrific rainstorm, and Ahab left quickly for Jezreel. [46] Then the LORD gave special strength to Elijah. He tucked his cloak into his belt and ran ahead of Ahab's chariot all the way to the

entrance of Jezreel **(I Kings 18 41-46 NLT).
Chapter 4, Page 47**

For I, the LORD your God, will hold your
right hand,
Saying to you, 'Fear not, I will help you'
(Isaiah 41:13 NKJV). Chapter 4, Page 48

Don't be selfish; don't try to impress
others. Be humble, thinking of others as
better than yourselves. Don't look out
only for your own interests, but take an
interest in others, too. You must have the
same attitude that Christ Jesus had.
(Philippians 2:3-5 NLT) Chapter 4, Page 49

And we are confident that he hears us
whenever we ask for anything that
pleases him. And since we know he hears
us when we make our requests, we also
know that he will give us what we ask for
(I John 5:14-15 (NLT). Chapter 4, Page 50

Give your burdens to the LORD, and he will take care of you. He will not permit the godly to slip and fall. **(Psalm 55:22 NLT).**
Chapter 5, Page 53

Look at the birds. They don't plant or harvest or store food in barns, for your heavenly Father feeds them. And aren't you far more valuable to him than they are? **(Matthew 6:26 NLT). Chapter 5, Page 54**

Be, still and know that I am God; I will be exalted among the nations, I will be exalted in the earth **(Psalm 46:10 NKJV).**
Chapter 5, Page 59

Walk with the wise and become wise; associate with fools and get in trouble **(Proverbs 13:20 NLT). Chapter 6, Page 63**

Don't team up with those who are unbelievers. How can righteousness be a partner with wickedness? How can light live with darkness? **(II Corinthians 6:14 NLT). Chapter 6, Page 64**

Then Peter took Him aside and began to rebuke Him, saying, "Far be it from You, Lord; this shall not happen to You!" But He turned and said to Peter, "Get behind Me, Satan! You are an offense to Me, for you are not mindful of the things of God, but the things of men" **(Matthew 16:22-23 NKJV). Chapter 6, Page 66**

But those who wait on the LORD
Shall renew *their* strength;
They shall mount up with wings like eagles,
They shall run and not be weary,
They shall walk and not faint **(Isaiah 40:31 NKJV). Chapter 7, Page 69**

"The vision is for an appointed time"
(Habakkuk 2:3 NKJV). Chapter 7, Page 71

And do not be conformed to this world,
but be transformed by the renewing of
your mind, that you may prove what *is*
that good and acceptable and perfect will
of God **(Romans 12:2 NKJV). Chapter 7,
Page 71**

And He said to me, "My grace is sufficient
for you, for My strength is made perfect in
weakness." Therefore most gladly I will
rather boast in my infirmities, that the
power of Christ may rest upon me. **(II
Corinthians 12:9 NKJV). Chapter 7, Page
73**

And my God shall supply all your need
according to His riches in glory by Christ
Jesus **(Philippians 4:19 NKJV). Chapter 7,
Page 74**

And Moses said to the people, "Do not be afraid. Stand still, and see the salvation of the L ORD , which He will accomplish for you today. For the Egyptians whom you see today, you shall see again no more forever. [14] The L ORD will fight for you, and you shall hold your peace."

And the L ORD said to Moses, "Why do you cry to Me? Tell the children of Israel to go forward. But lift up your rod, and stretch out your hand over the sea and divide it. And the children of Israel shall go on dry *ground* through the midst of the sea. And I indeed will harden the hearts of the Egyptians, and they shall follow them. So I will gain honor over Pharaoh and over all his army, his chariots, and his horsemen. Then the Egyptians shall know that I *am* the L ORD , when I have gained honor for

Myself over Pharaoh, his chariots, and his horsemen."

And the Angel of God, who went before the camp of Israel, moved and went behind them; and the pillar of cloud went from before them and stood behind them **(Exodus 14:13-19 NKJV). Chapter 7, Page 77**

But seek first the kingdom of God and His righteousness, and all these things shall be added to you **(Matthew 6:33 NKJV). Chapter 7, Page 77**

Humble yourselves before the Lord, and he will lift you up in honor **(James 4:10 NLT). Chapter 7, Page 78**

That is what the Scriptures mean when they say,

"No eye has seen, no ear has heard,
and no mind has imagined
what God has prepared
for those who love him" **(1 Corinthians 2:9 NLT). Chapter 7, Page 79**

Yet in all these things we are more than conquerors through Him who loved us **(Romans 8:37 NKJV). Chapter 7, Page 82**

Therefore, put on every piece of God's armor so you will be able to resist the enemy in the time of evil. Then after the battle you will still be standing firm. Stand your ground, putting on the belt of truth and the body armor of God's righteousness. For shoes, put on the peace that comes from the Good News so that you will be fully prepared. In addition to all of these, hold up the shield of faith to stop the fiery arrows of the devil. Put on salvation as your helmet, and take the

sword of the Spirit, which is the word of God. Pray in the Spirit at all times and on every occasion. Stay alert and be persistent in your prayers for all believers everywhere **(Ephesians 6:13-18 NLT).**
Chapter 8, Page 86

To everything there is a season,
A time for every purpose under heaven
(Ecclesiates 3:1 NKJV) Chapter 9, Page 89

Now after six days Jesus took Peter, James, and John his brother, led them up on a high mountain by themselves; and He was transfigured before them. His face shone like the sun, and His clothes became as white as the light **(Matthew 17:1-2 NKJV). Chapter 9, Page 91**

Trust in the LORD with all your heart,
And lean not on your own understanding
(Proverbs 3:5 NKJV). Chapter 10, Page 97

The LORD is good to those who depend on him, to those who search for him **(Lamentations 3:25 NLT). Chapter 10, Page 100**

What shall we say about such wonderful things as these? If God is for us, who can ever be against us? **(Romans 8:31 NLT). Chapter 10, Page 101**

Your own ears will hear him. Right behind you a voice will say, "This is the way you should go," whether to the right or to the left. **(Isaiah 30:21 NLT) Chapter 11, Page 103**

They won't follow a stranger; they will run from him because they don't know his voice" **(John 10:5 NLT). Chapter 11, Page 104**

It is better to trust in the LORD
Than to put confidence in man **(Psalm
118:8 NKJV). Chapter 11, Page 104**

And they overcame him by the blood of
the Lamb and by the word of their
testimony, and they did not love their
lives to the death. **Revelation 12:11
(NKJV). Chapter 12, Page 111**

No weapon formed against you shall
prosper,
And every tongue *which* rises against you
in judgment
You shall condemn.
This *is* the heritage of the servants of the
LORD,
And their righteousness *is* from Me,"
Says the LORD **(Isaiah 54:17 NKJV).
Chapter 12, Page 113**

Trust in the LORD with all your heart; do not depend on your own understanding. Seek his will in all you do, and he will show you which path to take **(Proverbs 3:5-6 NLT). Chapter 13, Page 117**

"Yes, come," Jesus said.

So Peter went over the side of the boat and walked on the water toward Jesus. But when he saw the strong wind and the waves, he was terrified and began to sink. "Save me, Lord!" he shouted.

Jesus immediately reached out and grabbed him. "You have so little faith," Jesus said. "Why did you doubt me?" **(Matthew 14:29-31 NLT). Chapter 13, Page 119**

In his kindness God called you to share in his eternal glory by means of Christ Jesus. So after you have suffered a little while, he will restore, support, and strengthen you, and he will place you on a firm foundation. **I Peter 5:10 (NLT) Chapter 14, Page 121**

When Jesus heard *that,* He said, "This sickness is not unto death, but for the glory of God, that the Son of God may be glorified through it" **(John 11:4 NKJV). Chapter 14, Page 123**

Be anxious for nothing, but in everything by prayer and supplication, with thanksgiving, let your requests be made known to God **(Philippians 4:6 NKJV). Chapter 15, Page 127**

If you openly declare that Jesus is Lord and believe in your heart that God raised him from the dead, you will be saved **(Romans 10:9 NLT). Invitation, Page 130**

Rather, you must grow in the grace and knowledge of our Lord and Savior Jesus Christ. All glory to him, both now and forever! Amen. **(II Peter 3:18 NLT). End, Page 150**

Don't be afraid, for I am with you.
Don't be discouraged, for I am your God.
I will strengthen you and help you.
I will hold you up with my victorious right hand (Isaiah 41:10 NLT). BONUS

HOW TO CONTACT THE AUTHOR

Satise Roddy is married and lives in a Minneapolis suburb with her husband Tim and their two cherished Siberian cats.

She is the founder and president of Satise Roddy Ministries, an Ordained Minister, Mentor, Speaker, Inspirational Speaker and Encourager. She also founded DESTINED WOMEN, a Women's Fellowship.

She is passionate about preaching the Word to inspire, encourage and empower others to walk in the freedom God has provided.

She is intentional about being a good steward of the temple God has entrusted her to, staying healthy spiritually, emotionally and physically. She enjoys running, ice skating and dancing and is an avid tea drinker.

She is passionate about her relationship with Jesus and guided by the Holy Spirit. God has put a song in her heart and her desire is to share it with the world, praying that all may come to know Him.

For speaking engagements, please contact the author at:

Satise Roddy Ministries
www.satiseroddy.com

Rather, you must grow in the grace and knowledge of our Lord and Savior Jesus Christ.

All glory to him, both now and forever! Amen. II Peter 3:18

You can always find me by visiting my website: www.satiseroddy.com

NOTES

NOTES

NOTES

NOTES

NOTES

NOTES